October 1999

Betty,

On behalf of the Mississippi Wildlife Federation, I want to wish you the very best in your retirement. You have been a tremendous asset to the Federation and all its affiliates. Thank you for your contribution in protecting the wild places that we all hold dear.

You will be missed -- but we hope to see you 'down South' soon!

Sincerely,
Marla Speed

WILD MISSISSIPPI
A NATURAL VIEW

EASTERN BOX TURTLE & BIRD'S FOOT VIOLETS
Tishomingo County, April 1992

WILD MISSISSIPPI

A NATURAL VIEW

STEPHEN KIRKPATRICK

INTRODUCTION BY
DAVID L. WATTS

WILD MISSISSIPPI
A NATURAL VIEW

Published by:

Thy Marvelous Works

P.O. Box 31414
Jackson, MS 39286

First Edition

Printed & bound by:
Arcata Graphics
Kingsport, TN

Color Separations by:
K & W Prepress
Jackson, MS

Designed by:
Sam Beibers

Edited by:
Ann Becker

Library of Congress Catalog
93-60295

ISBN # 0-9619353-6-7

(Preceding Pages) MOUNTAIN LAUREL & SPRING WATER
Stone County, April 1993

Dedication

To my wife, Marian,
and my sons, Sean, Ryan and Ian.
The time spent in the wonder of creation
draws us nearer to our Lord Jesus,
which in turn draws us nearer to each other.

WOLF RIVER SUNRISE
Harrison County, April 1993

To all those who have helped me over the years, I thank you. To you who have gone above and beyond the call of duty, my deepest gratitude:

Cliff Covington, Bobby McCain & Robbie Howell.

No one could accomplish much without the support of loved ones:

Mr. & Mrs. Ted Hoz, Mr. & Mrs. Shaw Enochs and Miss Susan Kirkpatrick. A special thanks to Mr. O. L. Kirkpatrick for giving me my first camera in 1981.

Also a word of thanks to:

Mississippi Wildlife Federation
Soil Conservation Service
MS Dept. of Wildlife, Fisheries & Parks
The Nature Conservancy
Cooperative Extension Service
Mississippi Forestry Commission
U.S. Dept. of the Interior
Natural Science Museum
Buffalo Peak Outfitters
LaCrosse Footwear

SUNRISE: COON'S VIEW
Madison County, January 1992

Preface

Communing with the natural world of Mississippi can be as easy as walking out the back door or glancing out the kitchen window. It can be as pleasurable as driving down the Natchez Trace Parkway. It can be as simple as wandering about a field of spring wildflowers on a crisp, clear day.

On the other hand, experiencing Mississippi's outdoors can sometimes be difficult and dangerous. Trudging through swamp for hours. Facing alligators neck-deep in creepy muck. Battling near frostbite or exhausting heat conditions.

Having roamed the Mississippi wilderness for years now, I know that my view of the outdoors has been somewhat varied. Always, the experience is enriching. The surprises have far outnumbered the expected. Every day out with nature has had some type of reward, not always in the form of photographs. My vision has been expanded, my eyes focused and senses tuned to all that is around me.

This state has much to offer. It is not like the west with its obvious, impressive expanses of great open spaces, glorious mountains with snow-capped peaks, and jagged cliffs pounded by stormy oceans. No, its beauty is more subtle, much like the people of Mississippi. We are somewhat quiet, peaceful, and slow-paced, and so is the natural world we inhabit. Ours is an intimate kind of wilderness, one to be sought out, discovered. Its offerings are all the more rich for our efforts. The view, once found, is unique and personal. Everchanging, Mississippi's natural beauty rewards us with a sense of privilege.

As we open our eyes to its offerings, the bounty of nature from one end of the state to the other is somewhat overwhelming. These pages are intended to inspire you, too, to wander into the woods or cross a stream or comb the beach at sunrise and see for yourself. In order to fully appreciate the wonders hidden there, however, you must do one thing. Give it a chance to warm up to you. Like its people, with their warm and giving spirit, the natural world of Mississippi will reward you with its own kind of Southern hospitality.

<u>GREAT EGRET OVERHEAD</u>
Madison County, April 1990

WEB & DEW
Stone County, May 1990

Contents

Our tendency is not to call things resources until the supply runs short.
When the end of the supply is in sight, we discover that the thing is valuable.
The next resource...is the wilderness.

Aldo Leopold, 1925

Introduction

by David L. Watts

*C*aution. Wildness ahead. The following photography may bring life-changing experiences to armchair naturalists. Proceed with compass and bug spray in hand.

"I slide my waders off the old walk log into the current and feel the press of cold water on warm flesh. In front of me, the chilled blue light of dawn climbs atop cypresses tipped in burnt umber and Indian yellow.... In moments to come, the imperceptible excitement of a new day gathers momentum. But I most notice the silence, broken only as falling acorns are baptized in black waters haloed by a morning mist." I first inscribed these words in my mind as I stood knee-deep in the most beautiful of east-central Mississippi's wild and free-flowing streams. I was completing a photo assignment for *Mississippi Outdoors*, the magazine where I earn my living. The utter silence and awe of those moments carefully chiseled sentiments of time and space into my conscience while anointing me with the waters of wild Mississippi.

Some people find it hard to imagine stretches of wild land in Mississippi. Maybe these are the urbanites longing for the vaster stretches of the Absarokas or perhaps the boreal regions of Canada's northwoods where they are sure there is plenty of primitiveness. They are searching for something I'm not sure they understand. One thing is for sure: They have never trudged with me along portions of the Black Creek Wilderness Area or wondered where they are on a cloudy day meandering through sloughs in the Big Swamp along the Pascagoula River. A few of them might not know wildness if it jumped right out of their quad maps.

To understand much about life in the Magnolia State is to know that Mississippians always have had strong attachments to the land and its untamed environs, its thick pine forests, hardwoods, and deep brooding riparian zones drained by picturesque stream courses. Today, these remote areas, those not in peril from backhoes and bulldozers, have become permanent fixtures in the lives of most of our citizens. For we have learned that the nature of flooded bottomland and coastal beach, loess bluff and black prairie helps prevent the erosion of our invaluable identities to place and time. Or, as George Friedrich Hegel said: "Life has a value only when it has something valuable as its object."

We are reminded by the brilliant artistry of Stephen Kirkpatrick's photographs in *Wild Mississippi* that our sense of community has been shaped in part by our state's natural and wildlife resources. For countless generations, these resources have nourished our consciences, even our physical well-beings. Perish the thought that my world in Mississippi could be denuded of rivers, trees, and birds.

For Mississippians – and I mean real Mississippians – the natural elements that span our five degrees of latitude are like powerful movements of great symphonies, stirring our imaginations and helping us lose ourselves at a moment's notice. The great natural forces dominating Mississippi's more than 47,000 square miles are the poetry of nature and a magical, healing elixir for the soul. Kirkpatrick has made these feelings and emotions seem bigger than life through the photographs in the pages to come.

Too bad that our lives often are divided into payroll periods. We are too often embroiled in incongruence, time spent with plastic people lacking a propriety for how to really enjoy life. Facing the stark realities of all this is a prescription for peace in the realm of Kirkpatrick's "Quiet

Waters." We're talking real retreats where truth is distilled from the damp mist at sunrise over a vast swamp. That "one impulse from a vernal wood...," as Wordsworth put it. Here lives a larger and simpler reality of great blue herons and moorhens, ringed sawbacks and nutria. Set against a sunrise warming a wetland fog is a soothing tonic of towhees and titmice that translates the healing balm of brute nature once removed from the smokestacks of our urban hinterlands.

For me, nature's beauty and comeliness cement themselves in my mind when I see the images of coastal expanse and the rugged, timeless purity of the barrier islands. I vividly recall that blustery February day 20 years ago when I stepped ashore on Horn Island for the first time. A shallow ledge had kept our boat 300 yards out, and I was faced with shedding too many clothes and wading ashore with my camera gear held overhead. Though I will never forget that sting of crotch-deep cold water in Mississippi Sound and the stout northwester that morning, I recall that my realization of wildness had succumbed to a mutation of life. What lay before me were not the grand processes of nature I had imagined, only the end product, a sense of natural beauty fleshed out for me by a primal experience.

Take a look at the photographs of "Coastal Sands" and see what I mean. Glimpse the fabric that binds rolling pine dunes and shrub scrub, brackish

GREAT BLUE HERON
Kemper County, April 1993

marsh and Gulf waters, all tied to the lives of brown pelicans, skimmers, and a host of shorebirds and neotropical migrants. Much like sea oats battling to anchor shifting sands against torrents of wind, water, and time, preventing their ever-so-slowly westward movement, coastal images become portraits of geologic time that have helped stabilize a valuable marine resource for everyone.

If Stephen Kirkpatrick's photography tells us anything, it is that our people seem to have a sense of stewardship for the bounty of creation surrounding us. From the sights and feelings evoked in "Open Spaces" and "Wooded Expanse," one senses that the care and nurture – call it love if you will – shown by man for the land has been returned by it to the venerable stewards. Can we expect any higher adulation?

Maybe not. But our responsibility is greater. Simply because so many hundreds of thousands of Mississippians assess the character of a priceless natural heritage as our most important endowment for the future. If Stephen Kirkpatrick's photographs can engender within us a deeper understanding of the natural order and our duties as custodians of a valuable natural and wildlife resource, then we can better position future generations of our citizens to inherit and pass on in perpetuity another chapter of wild Mississippi.

David L. Watts, Editor
Mississippi Outdoors
April 1993

BALD EAGLE
Issaquena County, November 1988

I. OPEN SPACES

Prairies, Meadows, Fields & Bogs

INDIAN BLANKETS
Forrest County, July 1991

I have never heard a butterfly's wings beating. I have followed close, trying, as they flutter from flower to flower in their silent dance. A rush of air pushes through, short-lived, and forces the flower to bow to the sky as the silent gathering of nectar goes on. But there is no sound.

I have often wondered how they do it, how butterflies cling to the flowers, that is. After another rush of air, the butterfly is off to the edge of the field, only to be replaced by another even more brilliant. It is a tiger swallowtail this time, hanging onto a beautiful lavender stokesia.

Here in Sweetbay Bog, owned by the Nature Conservancy of Mississippi, I have often lost track of time in search of photographic opportunities in this rich ecosystem. The diversity of flora and fauna in a bog like this is staggering. Here the very rare Grass of Parnassus grows. This is one of only about 20 places in the entire world this plant can be found. This Grass shares its space with other natural gems of the bog such as Grass-Pink Orchid, Rose Pogonia, and carnivorous specimens like pitcher plants and sundews. You might even discover a Snowy Orchid if you are persistent and observant.

I once stumbled across a bog in Harrison County that was very large and had an abundance of Thread-Leaf Sundew growing in it. As I wandered around the bog, careful not to crush any plant life underfoot, I found a spot I liked and settled in. Slumped over, consumed with photographing the bounty before me, I stayed. After a while I "came up for air" and noticed a man coming toward me from the road. He was an older gentleman, and as he approached I went to meet him.

We introduced ourselves and began to talk. I explained why I was there and my absorption in what was before us. I learned that this man owned the land and his house was the one I could see nearby. Also I learned that he had no knowledge of what he was now standing in as I pointed out, with a great deal of enthusiasm, the different types of plant life to which he played host.

We became friendly and within a few moments he, like most older people I often meet, began to tell me a story from his past. His eyes lit up as he said, "You reminded me of a fellow I used to see out here years ago when I was a boy. A young man would ride his bicycle down that road there, which used to be gravel, and park it near the edge of the grass. He would walk into the bog about where we are standing now and set up an old canvas stool and an easel. He would sit there and paint, sometimes all day."

"Did he come here often?" I asked.

"Often enough that my mother warned me to stay away from him. He would just draw and paint all day."

"I guess this beautiful bog would inspire people," I said as I began to point out different dew-covered plants in the warm, early morning light. He began to take notice.

"It is pretty," he said. "I've never really looked at this place that way before."

"I guess if your mother were here you would not have come near me today," I said with a smile.

He smiled back. "You artist types are strange."

"I'm not an artist, I'm a photographer."

"Oh. Oh yes, that's right."

"You don't mind if I stay out here and shoot some more, do you?"

"No, go right ahead. Stay all day if you like." He turned and headed for his car as I gazed out over the field. I could see how someone like the man he had described could be caught up in this beauty for hours. Then it hit me. Gautier, Mississippi. Strange artist.

I turned and called to the gentleman. "Hey, by the way, do you know who that fellow was who used to sit out here and paint?"

He turned. "Yeah, his name was Walter Anderson."

"Walter Anderson. Really. The painter."

"He sat about where you are now." He smiled a broad smile, then turned and headed to the road.

I smiled and looked down as the past telescoped into the present. It gave me a good feeling. Loudly I called back to him, "Does that mean I'm a strange artist type?"

Without turning he replied, "No, you're a photographer."

TIGER SWALLOWTAIL ON STOKESIA
Stone County, May 1991

FOG, FOXTAILS & SUNRAYS
Madison County, October 1990

HORSE NETTLE SEED PODS IN FOXTAILS
Madison County, December 1992

WHITE-TAILED DEER LEAPING
Issaquena County, February 1989

<u>BLACK WILLOW AT SUNRISE</u>
Madison County, December 1991

KINGBIRD & YOUNG
Madison County, July 1991

CRIMSON CLOVER AT RESERVOIR
Madison County, April 1992

HUMMINGBIRD MOTH AT BLAZING STAR
Madison County, October 1991

GRASS-PINK ORCHIDS & DEW
Stone County, May 1992

The Mississippi Flyway is the champion of migratory routes for birds. It covers our state as the mighty Mississippi River guides its path. Waterfowl in great numbers follow its lead right into the heart of the Delta. Populations of ducks and geese soar during the winter months in this rich, wet farmland area of our state.

SNOW & BLUE GEESE AT DUSK
Washington County, January 1992

<u>CLOUD COVER AT SUNRISE</u>
Lawrence County, January 1990

Opposite: *The Mississippi sandhill crane is a nonmigratory subspecies of the sandhill crane. It is an endangered species, with fewer than 135 individuals and a dozen breeding pairs. This large, majestic bird has one of the most thrilling calls you will hear in the wild. Here they are performing what is known as a "unison call." The adult birds pictured here are with their year-old offspring. Within the entire Gulf Coast refuge, an average of only one chick per year survives. This is a ten-year trend which may change in 1993, as several chicks have recently hatched and are doing well.*

MISSISSIPPI SANDHILL CRANES
Jackson County, January 1993

22 EASTERN WILD TURKEY GOBBLERS
Covington County, December 1990

Mississippi has become famous for its turkey hunting. The state has more than 500,000 Eastern wild turkeys within its borders. The spring ritual of "strutting and gobbling" has sent many an observer's blood pressure soaring. The experience is one not soon forgotten. Even from the roads of Mississippi, turkey sightings are a common occurrence.

NINE-BANDED ARMADILLO
Issaquena County, May 1988

BOBOLINK CALLING IN VETCH
Warren County, April 1992

SUNRISE & FOG
Warren County, October 1992

SOUTHERN BLUE FLAG & TREE FROG
Madison County, April 1991

RED-WINGED BLACKBIRD AT SUNSET
Rankin County, February 1992

BLACK & YELLOW ARGIOPE AND DEW
Stone County, September 1991

*Most people know little about Red Bluff.
Situated near Morgantown on Highway 587,
the unusual layers of clay make it a point of
interest for all who pass by. Take a hike down to
the wooded areas below and you will find a
wealth of flora, fauna, and cool spring waters.
Venture out even farther to the Pearl River, and
you will easily spend an entire day taking in the
natural sights.*

RED BLUFF & PINE TREE
Marion County, February 1993

BLACKBERRIES
Holmes County, June 1991

Opposite: RED-WINGED BLACKBIRDS
Tallahatchie County, January 1988

HERMIT CRAB
Jackson County, March 1991

II. COASTAL SANDS

Gulf Coast & Barrier Islands

DRIFTWOOD AT SUNSET
Jackson County, March 1991

I wiggled my toes in the sand. The lapping rhythm of the waves soothed me, and porpoises blew their spray nearby. The cool breeze made me rub my arms for warming friction as the sun, glowing as a halo formed around it, dropped on the horizon. Ship Island looked small next to the fiery ball. It was awe-inspiring. I quickly began to shoot, frame after frame, hoping to capture the fleeting vision as it vanished all too soon. It seemed as though the Gulf of Mexico had consumed it.

"Dad, hey Dad." The quiet was broken as two of my sons ran up from behind. "Let's go." They had been playing pirates for days, still enthusiastic in spite of having yet to discover any buried treasure. They loved coming here to Horn Island each year. Five days of camping out in primitive conditions does us all a world of good.

On this trip the osprey woke us each morning with their screaming cry at 5:30 a.m. There is no better alarm clock. As I got up I saw the others simply roll over and burrow deeper into their sleeping bags. I headed out to do my morning photography. Early and late were about the only times to shoot. The light during the day, for the most part, was far too harsh. The abundance of water and white sand only magnified the problem.

As with all things in life, there are negatives to camping on Horn Island. Here, if you do not like sand in everything, you ought not come. But far worse are the bugs. Mosquitoes, sand flies, and gnats can be absolutely the death of a trip here. The Lord's blessings were with us this time; a cold front had blown through upon our arrival, bringing with it blue sky, cool temperatures, and a constant wind to control the bugs.

I gathered up my gear. This had been a memorable evening. We headed back to the camp site. The boys were asking their usual "Twenty Questions." My friend Steve Joyce and his son, Charlie, were there as we arrived. We got our evening driftwood fire going as we prepared to eat and restore our liquids. Water is at a premium here since you have to bring it all from the mainland, as with everything else. Gulping down Kool-Aid is not allowed!

That night supper seemed especially good. We fried some white bass I had brought along for a special meal. The boys finished first, as always, and restlessly poked the fire while Steve and I tried to savor the quietude of the night. "Go off and follow the trail," I told them in an attempt to quiet our surroundings. Off they went, flashlights lighting their path. "Brave of them," I thought to myself, as the silence of the outdoors returned. Sean and Charlie were 7 and Ryan was 5.

The twilight was giving way to a brilliant full moon. You could count every star in the clear, black sky. Soon Steve and I began to clean up after supper, quietly talking.

It wasn't long before our three explorers returned, somewhat ecstatic and firing off questions. "What color are their eyes?" Ryan asked.

"Are they red?" Sean exclaimed.

BOTTLE-NOSED DOLPHIN WITH MULLET
Harrison County, February 1989

"Because we saw some red eyes!" all three shouted.

"Wait, what eyes? What eyes are you talking about?" I asked.

"The red wolf," all three again chorused.

"Will they eat us?" Charlie asked, his fear of my answer showing mostly through his eyes.

The red wolf was introduced to Horn Island several years ago and the breeding program has been quite successful. Because of the size and location of the island, this is a perfect place to keep the wolves under wraps while they are being studied. I had told the story of the red wolf

wanted a wolf to howl about now!

"So," I said, "if you see a wolf, you should raise up one leg. Bend it at the knee and keep it behind you." I demonstrated. "When he sees you, it looks like he has already eaten your leg,

around the fire were syrupy.

Soon a request came. "Will y'all come with us to find some?" I was so amazed by the question I don't remember who asked it. I thought after that explanation, no one would dare venture out into the dark.

SUNSET HALO NEAR SHIP ISLAND
Harrison County, March 1992

to the boys and they really wanted to see one.

Now, in between all their questions, I was trying to explain how not to get eaten by wolves.

"A wolf will only attack you one time." I told them. Eyes were wide as they watched and listened. "If they think they have gotten you before, they won't hurt you again." Their silence was tense and unusual for these three. The crackling fire only added to the drama. Oh, how I

and he won't come after you."

The looks coming from those faces cannot be put into words. They seemed to be practicing this maneuver in their minds as all three slowly swallowed at the same time. I said nothing else. Steve looked over at me and we both became stone-faced. The next few moments passed slowly. Even the boys' movements

"No, go by yourselves," I answered. They would have no part of it, so all five of us headed out to find the red wolf.

We didn't go far when I stopped abruptly. "There. See those red eyes?" I didn't see anything, but three flashlights were immediately all pointed straight ahead. Silence dominated.

"Where?" a squeaky voice finally asked.

"Right there." I said. Light beams were focused straight ahead, all concentrated on the brush before us, illuminating the night, motionless.

Soon the beams of light became very unsteady and began to move about everywhere in the trees. What was the problem? I turned toward the boys. I saw the three of them, each unsteady, standing flamingolike on one leg. Trying to balance themselves in the sand, they all soon had raised legs moving like pump handles in frantic maneuvers.

It was all I could do to keep a straight face. "Let's move on," I suggested. "Let's see if we can find something else."

After a few quiet moments passed, a young voice asked, "Were you joking? Is that true about a wolf not getting us if we hold up our leg?"

In the darkness my face didn't give me away. I was grinning from ear to ear. "Did the wolf get you?" I asked.

"No," a voice replied.

"Then," I said, "it must work."

ROYAL TERNS & LAUGHING GULLS
Harrison County, April 1993

HORN ISLAND COASTLINE
Jackson County, March 1991

HORN ISLAND SUNRISE
Jackson County, March 1992

BLACK WIDOW
Jackson County, April 1992

YAUPON
Jackson County, March 1991

SUNRISE AT LOW TIDE, HORN ISLAND
Jackson County, March 1992

OSPREY AT SUNRISE
Jackson County, March 1992

SEA OATS AT SUNSET
Harrison County, July 1991

GULLS AT SUNRISE
Jackson County, March 1992

SEASHELLS
Jackson County, March 1991

BLACK SKIMMERS IN FLIGHT
Harrison County, August 1989

SEA NETTLE & FIDDLER CRAB
Hancock County, June 1991

DRIFTWOOD AT DAWN
Harrison County, April 1993

GHOST CRAB HOLE & VEGETATION
Jackson County, March 1991

SEASIDE BALM
Jackson County, March 1991

Seaside Balm (Conradina canescen) is a member of the mint family and probably the plant hardest to find in the state. The only place it has been discovered is in one tiny area of Horn Island. Humbly I admit that when I came across them, I saw only pretty flowers. Little did I know I had photographed a state treasure.

SOUTHERN LEOPARD FROG
Jackson County, March 1992

HORN ISLAND SUNSET
Jackson County, July 1991

EASTERN SCREECH OWL
Madison County, January 1991

III. WOODED EXPANSE

Forests & Woods

TREES IN LATE LIGHT
Claiborne County, July 1990

As I sat on the old stump, my body shook. Tears rolled down my face. I could see them in the dead leaves beneath me as I cradled my head in my hands. Crying out to the Lord, I again and again asked for strength. A gentle breeze made me look up from time to time as if I were going to see an answer before me. Most of my time in this place was without words.

I often came here to the woods to work through my hurts. I desperately wanted to continue on with my photography, but nothing seemed to be going right. The financial and emotional pressure was killing me.

As I wandered the wooded expanse behind our house and sat on that old stump, I acquired a calmness and the sense of hope I needed to carry on. The songs of the birds mixed with the melody of the wind called to my heart. A quietly flowing stream sang a rhapsody of love, feeding my soul.

I know I was no closer to God out there than I was in the house, but this natural classroom had a chalkboard I could understand. Day after day I became more sensitive to its message. Often I would put down my camera and just observe for hours, never taking a single photograph. We had no money, no job prospects, and criticism from every side, but I had heard the Lord's call. I knew I must withstand the trial

62

before me with commitment and faith if I were ever to amount to anything. I also knew I had a long way to go to even be an acceptable photographer and an even longer way to go to grasp all the secrets of these wonderful woods.

That winter of 1984-1985 was the pivotal time in my photography career. Our electricity was turned

HERMIT THRUSH CALLING
Copiah County, February 1988

off because we could not pay a $47 bill. My wife and I were tested through trial after trial, but we came through those difficult times better off. Our lives now are bonded together, my business's foundation was poured in concrete, and lessons were learned that no school could teach me. Those were some of the most memorable times of my life.

Often I still go to the woods when my heart is heavy, because I know it will be lighter when I leave. As I search the woods for the photographs that will touch people or illustrate nature's

miracle, the setting usually ministers to me instead. Searching out those special moments and places can be very rewarding. Physical challenges as well as mental ones can make the endeavor demanding as well. In the woods, searching for the perfect photograph is more complicated than in fields and rivers because there are so many more areas to cover. Things are under your feet, over your head, and all about you. Trying to see it all can be difficult. Attempting to photograph it is even harder, especially when you add light conditions that are broken, uneven, and sometimes very dark.

I think about the photographers who don't even bother to go to the woods. They are missing out on beauty without measure. Every so often a scene appears before me that cannot be put into words. As my mind wanders and my eyes scan everywhere, suddenly there it is, the perfect setting. As I stop to shoot and survey the possibilities, I again experience the calmness of my Mississippi woods. The dogwoods, cool streams, calling birds, and ever-so-precious quiet that exists here cannot be replaced with anything the city has to offer. Again I catch myself sitting back, leaving the cameras for the moment, and taking another lesson from the finest classroom I have ever entered.

For me, it is not enough to simply view the woods; they must be experienced. I must venture in. I must become part of it in order to see and hear what is being taught. As I walked in some woods one day with my two boys, their questions, as always, were probing.

"Where are we going in the woods, Dad?" Sean asked.

"Looking for things," I answered.

"Is it far from here?" Ryan asked.

"Maybe," I said.

"Don't you know where we are going?" Ryan said, confused.

I tried to explain. "I don't know what the Lord has for us today. We'll have to see."

"This is God's house, isn't it, Dad?" Sean asked.

"No Sean, God is everywhere, isn't that right, Dad?" Ryan challenged.

I said nothing for a few minutes as I looked about and continued to walk. I felt His presence all around in the wonder of the cool autumn evening. I was happy to be able to spend time in the wild with my sons, and this conversation only reinforced my outdoor schooling and brought back memories of a certain stump in a certain woods.

"You're both right," I answered, slowly.

"We are?" they said together.

My eyes grew wide and my heart was full as I answered. "Isn't that something? We are in His house, and He is everywhere!"

DOGWOODS ON LITTLE SAND CREEK
Claiborne County, March 1993

CHOCOLATE LENZITES ON BRANCH
Madison County, January 1992

OKTOC CREEK
Noxubee County, December 1992

BOTTOMLAND HARDWOOD SUNRISE
Madison County, December 1991

PROTHONOTARY WARBLER
Washington County, April 1992

FALL COLORS
Wilkinson County, November 1992

EASTERN NARROW-MOUTHED TOAD
Smith County, May 1992

If you decide to look for Lady Slipper Orchids in Mississippi, you better have some help. They have a short flowering season and only grace a very few wooded slopes in the northeast and east central sections of the state. Of this grouping of 11 plants I counted 14 blooms. I was ecstatic when I found them; photographing them was one of the most moving experiences I have had in the natural world. My three-year search for them had finally been rewarded.

YELLOW LADY'S SLIPPER ORCHIDS
Lee County, May 1993

PREDACIOUS STINKBUG ON CICADA
Hinds County, September 1991

RACCOON SKULL
Madison County, February 1992

WATERFALL AT SUNSET
Tishomingo County, April 1993

Most people think of babbling brooks when they think of moving water in Mississippi. However, some rather impressive waterfalls are scattered across the state. Here, the layers of shale make for a memorable scene in the wild near Pickwick Lake. For me, the soothing sounds and cool, clear water calmed a somewhat hectic day.

EASTERN WILD TURKEY AT ROOST
Claiborne County, February 1991

YOUNG RACCOONS
Issaquena County, July 1988

YELLOW JESSAMINE
Claiborne County, March 1992

<u>PERSIMMONS</u>
Montgomery County, October 1992

YOUNG FERAL HOG
Stone County, February 1993

Being nocturnal, the feral or wild hog is a little-seen animal of the Mississippi wilds. Even though they are short on sight, the hogs' very sensitive ears and noses make any approach by another animal or a human nearly impossible. This young hog doesn't carry the long, dangerous tusks of the adult boar, but he is still not something you would want to run into in the darkness.

GRAY SQUIRRELS PLAYING
Hinds County, March 1990

CHICKASAW PLUM BLOOMS AT DUSK
Claiborne County, March 1993

DIAMONDBACK RATTLESNAKE
George County, September 1992

DARLING UNDERWING ON HICKORY
Hancock County, April 1991

<u>CARDINAL IN REDBUD</u>
Montgomery County, April 1993

CINNAMON FERNS & LICHEN
Hancock County, April 1993

BIGLEAF MAGNOLIA
Kemper County, April 1993

Mention white-tailed deer in Mississippi and heads turn. It is certainly the most popular game species in the state as well as one sought out by photographers and nature lovers alike. With a population estimated at some 3 million animals, white-tailed deer outnumber humans by nearly half a million.

WHITE-TAILED DEER
Issaquena County, March 1989

<u>SUNRISE OVER PINES</u>
George County, September 1992

WATER MOCCASIN
Madison County, September 1991

IV. QUIET WATERS

Rivers, Creeks, Lakes & Reservoirs

FOGGY SUNRISE ON PEARL RIVER
Madison County, September 1991

Quite frankly I was glad the evening was over. It had been a long five days. With four programs for the Soil Conservation Service, each in a different city, and three days of shooting, I was worn out. Now all I had to do was pack up the equipment, load it in my Jeep, and drive four hours home.

those pictures we saw in the program tonight." He was referring to my multimedia slide show, "The Harmony of Nature."

"Well," I said, "my equipment is better than it used to be."

"Yeah," he said with a nod. "I don't have the money for the

Only two things really give you a photo, the film and the lens. The camera just holds these two together."

"I never thought of it that way before, but I guess you're right."

"Are you familiar with a print of mine called 'Heart's Desire'?"

AMERICAN COOTS & FOG AT SUNRISE
Madison County, October 1986

As I was putting away my projectors, a young man came up to me. He was very direct. "I do a little photography and was wondering if you could answer a few questions."

"Sure," I answered.

"You must have some really expensive equipment to take

really good stuff. But I do have a little 35mm with a zoom lens."

"That's all you need. A camera, a lens, some film, and get after it. Does your camera work?"

"Works fine. But it's not fancy."

"That's okay. A camera's nothing but an expensive film holder.

"Yes, sir. The one with the deer running through the swamp. It's my favorite." His face lit up. In Mississippi, if you want to hit on most men's favorite subject, just bring up deer.

"Well, that photograph was taken with less than $500 worth of equipment, including film."

I could see on his face that his mind was racing to the deer stand in the morning. All things were possible now. But then doubt crept back in. "A lot of the really good pictures are taken in other states, though. You need to travel to get to good places."

"No," I answered. "The best place to do your most creative photo-graphy is in your own backyard."

He paused a moment. "Where is your favorite place to take pictures?" he asked.

I thought for a moment as every place I had been under the sun passed through my memory. Then it hit me. "Mississippi," I answered with a smile.

"Really? Why?"

"Because I know it better than anywhere else I could go." Of course, for a long time, Mississippi was the only place I could afford to go.

"Do you have a favorite place here?"

Now that was a hard question. But I had the answer. "The Pearl River Swamp on the north end of Ross Barnett Reservoir." The very thought of the place brought back memories by the hundreds.

ALLIGATOR
Madison County, March 1991

"Ever have anything unusual happen out there? Don't you get in the water and stuff? I could never do that."

Many wonderful things have happened to me in that place, and many wonderful photographs have come from there, but for some reason, what came to mind was the single

worst day I ever had in the swamp.

I began my story. "I really thought it was going to be one of those perfect mornings. As I stood near the water's edge, I could hear the swamp coming alive. In the distance, I could hear the call of ducks. Ducks are my favorite subject.

"I was dressing in the dark, trying to get my wet suit on. It was October, and the air kept me cool while I worked to get it on. Finally, I stepped off into the swamp and moved toward the cattails, camera in hand, film on my head, and camouflage covering me and my float.

"Now I was at what I call 'frog's-eye view.' The cold from the muck was seeping through my suit. As the sun started to show, I spotted some coots in the distance, so I worked my way toward them. As I got closer I moved slower and slower, but finally they exploded into the air. I laid my finger on the camera's trigger to shoot a series, and after one shot there was total silence. Nothing. I had run out of film. I had committed the worst mistake in photography, which is not knowing where you are on a roll.

"I rewound and changed film. In this setup that was no easy chore. Just as I suspected, the coots' action was over by the time I was ready. I was sick. But I got my composure back just as the coots started stirring again. This never happens. So I shot several more frames before the coots were gone for good. I had gotten a second chance.

"I drifted on through the swamp water and spotted some wood ducks in the lilies. This time, before I got any closer, I checked my roll, and it was near the end. I rewound it and was trying to get it out of the camera when I heard a terrible sound. "Bloop!" The film dropped into the water and out of sight.

"My heart sank. My coots were gone. You know why I got upset, don't you? Because when your family eats from the sale of

photos, special moments are of extreme importance to survival.

"The next hour passed as I

FLOATING ORCHID
Madison County, September 1992

pushed my muskrat blind through the snags and lotus plants. I took random photographs of various subjects in the morning light. I was still very upset about losing the film and had considered returning to my Jeep and calling it a day several times. But then I

spotted the wood ducks I had seen earlier and decided to try to get near them. It wasn't long before I had forgotten about the coots and was totally focused on the woodies.

"I got closer and closer and they never seemed to even look up. They were eating among the lilies and I got some great shots. I stayed with them a long while, mostly waiting for interesting moments and light. It was now up in the day. Clouds were rolling in, bringing shade. The air had warmed up some, but the water was starting to chill me. It was time to head in.

"As I headed back on the hour-long trip to shore, I spotted something and headed toward it. I could see as I got closer that it was a ring-necked duck. I took a couple of shots and finished another roll.

"The duck seemed content, so I slowly removed the roll and stored it in the bag on my head. I was putting a new roll of film into the back of the camera when all of a sudden the most forceful thrust I have ever felt rammed my leg beneath the water. Tons of water exploded into the air and my face. I went face down into the swamp. The force launched my camera and my film into oblivion. I saw a large, black, scaly shape and knew it was an alligator. I tried to regain my balance and all I could think about was the alligator, the camera, the film, my leg, my life.

"Then as quickly as it happened, it was over. Dead calm. I stared out over the swamp while water drained off my head. Then, right in front of me, was my green film bag, floating. The film inside was safe in airtight containers. I started to look for my camera. I had to look for awhile, but I did locate it. The camera and lens were wet and covered in lily roots. Needless to say, I was sick. I had lost another roll of film.

"As it turned out, however, the one coot shot from the first roll came out, along with some good wood duck and ring-neck duck shots. It was a memorable day of photographing Mississippi."

"Has anything like that ever happened since?" he asked. I could tell he wasn't sure if he really wanted to know.

"No, I have never had another

RINGED SAWBACK IN PEARL RIVER
Madison County, June 1991

The Ringed Sawback Turtle is unique to the Pearl River System; that is, the Pearl River is the only place in the entire world where it can be found. Ongoing studies of this endangered species continue to reveal more about its habits and habitat.

gator ram me, but from time to time large fish get squeezed between my legs. You can bet that will get your attention."

"I think I would die if that

happened to me," he said, shaking his head. "Well, I need to let you go. Can I help you with anything?"

"No, I can get it." I paused. "You going to go and take some photos tomorrow?"

"No," he answered. "Think I'll sleep in tomorrow."

"Aw, come on. You've got to get out there and take those photos."

"You're too serious. I can't handle that. Besides, all that wasn't made for us fat boys." He smiled as he slapped his slightly protruding belly, then turned to leave.

"I know something that will help you get that off," I said with a grin.

He stopped. "What's that?"

"One good-sized gar fish!"

<u>SNOWY EGRET TOSSING SHAD</u>
Issaquena County, July 1988

Wading birds are abundant in the state and seem to be a favorite among photographers. I suppose their somewhat exotic appearance is the reason. These birds use many methods for catching fish, but only one method works when it comes to swallowing them, and that is "head first." If they don't eat their catch head first, fins and scales will hang up in the birds' throats. Here, a shad is being tossed into position for the long trip down the neck.

Black Creek is the only National Wild and Scenic River in the state. It runs through Lamar, Forrest, Perry, Stone, and George Counties before entering the Pascagoula River. The wonderful scenery and fast-moving, deep water of Black Creek make it the most popular float trip in Mississippi. Fishing, photography, camping, and just enjoying nature are more than reason enough to visit it.

BLACK CREEK & MOUNTAIN LAUREL
Perry County, May 1993

FALL CYPRESS TREE
Rankin County, October 1991

PASCAGOULA RIVER AT SUNRISE
Jackson County, May 1991

CYPRESS SWAMP REFLECTIONS
Madison County, April 1991

ANHINGA IN FLIGHT
Madison County, June 1990

STORM CLOUDS OVER MISSISSIPPI RIVER
Claiborne County, February 1992

RIVER OTTER
Madison County, September 1987

BAYOU CASTELLE REFLECTIONS
Jackson County, May 1992

COMMON MOORHEN & CHICK
Madison County, July 1991

SUNSET SILHOUETTES
Madison County, November 1992

WOOD DUCKS ON WILLOW LIMB
Claiborne County, December 1992

LILY PADS AT SUNSET
Jackson County, March 1991

SNOW ON CHUNKY RIVER
Clarke County, March 1993

BLUE CRAYFISH
Stone County, April 1993

Blue crayfish are somewhat of an aberration of nature similar to albinism. This also occurs occasionally in lobsters.

WINTER CYPRESS SLOUGH
Warren County, January 1993

<u>ROOTS AT SUNSET</u>
Madison County, December 1987

CLAPPER RAIL
Hancock County, January 1992

CHICKASAWHAY RIVER AT SUNRISE
Wayne County, February 1992

NUTRIA FAMILY
Quitman County, February 1993

BROAD-BANDED WATER SNAKE
Washington County, April 1992

SWAMP SUNSET
Madison County, January 1991

Photo Facts

All photographs in this book were taken with Nikon F3 & F4S cameras. I also use a Bogen 3221 tripod. The moments captured were not altered with filters, flash or computer manipulation. All shots were in the wild under natural conditions in natural light. I have tried to keep the photos as true to the scene as possible. I will admit, however, that I have gone to great extremes to be in the right place at the right time in the right light!

Page #	Lens	Exposure	Film	Support
1	105mm	1/60 @ f8	Velvia	Handheld
2-3	24mm	1/2 @ f16	Velvia	Tripod
5	24mm	1/30 @ f4	Velvia	Handheld
6	24mm	1/4 @ f22	Velvia	Tree
7	400mm	1/1000 @ f3.5	Fuji 50	Handheld
8-9	105mm	1/8 @ f16	Velvia	Tripod
11	400mm	1/500 @ f4	Velvia	Handheld
12	24mm	1/30 @ f11	Velvia	Tripod
13	400mm	1/1000 @ f4	KR 64	Handheld
15	105mm	1/60 @ f8	Velvia	Handheld
16	50mm	1/60 @ f11	KR 64	Handheld
17	105mm	1/8 @ f22	Velvia	Tripod
18	400mm	1/1000 @ f3.5	KR 64	Handheld
19	50mm	1 sec. @ f16	Velvia	Tripod
20	400mm	1/250 @ f5.6	Velvia	Handheld
21	24mm	1/8 @ f16	Velvia	Tripod
22	105mm	1/60 @ f8	Velvia	Handheld
23	105mm	1/2 @ f22	Velvia	Tripod
24-25	400mm	1/500 @ f8	Velvia	Handheld
26	50mm	1/8 @ f11	KR 64	Tripod
27	400mm & 1.4 teleconverter			
		1/250 @ f3.5	Velvia	Tripod
28	400mm	1/250 @ f4	KR 64	Tripod
29	400mm	1/125 @ f4	KR 64	Monopod
30	400mm & 1.4 teleconverter			
		1/250 @ f4	Velvia	Handheld
31	105mm	1/125 @ f16	Velvia	Handheld
32	105mm	1/30 @ f11	Velvia	Tripod
33	400mm	1/500 @ f11	Velvia	Handheld
34	105mm	1/30 @ f16	Velvia	Tripod
35	24mm	4 sec. @ f22	Velvia	Tripod
36	400mm	1/500 @ f4	KR 64	Monopod
37	105mm	1/8 @ f22	Velvia	Tripod
38	105mm	1/8 @ f16	Velvia	Tripod
39	105mm	1/125 @ f16	KR 64	Handheld
40	300mm	1/500 @ f5.6	KR 64	Handheld
41	400mm	1/250 @ f11	Velvia	Tripod
42	400 & 1.4 teleconverter			
		1/500 @ f4	Velvia	Tripod
43	24mm	1/15 @ f22	KR 64	Tripod
44-45	50mm	1/4 @ f22	KR 64	Tripod
46	105mm	1/30 @ f11	Velvia	Tripod
47	105mm	1/15 @ f16	Velvia	Tripod
48	24mm	1/8 @ f22	Velvia	Tripod
49	400mm	1/250 @ f4	Velvia	Handheld
50	50mm	1/15 @ f16	Velvia	Tripod
51	400mm	1/250 @ f4	Velvia	Monopod
52	50mm	1/60 @ f16	Velvia	Handheld
53	400mm	1/1000 @ f3.5	KR 64	Handheld
54	105mm	1/8 @ f16	KR 64	Tripod
55	400mm	1/250 @ f3.5	Velvia	Monopod
56	24mm	1/4 @ f22	KR 64	Tripod
57	105mm	1/8 @ f11	Velvia	Tripod
58	105mm	1/4 @ f22	Velvia	Tripod
59	50mm	1/15 @ f22	Velvia	Tripod
60	50mm	1/30 @ f11	Velvia	Tripod
61	400mm	1/125 @ f5.6	Velvia	Tripod
62	400mm	1/250 @ f5.6	KR 64	Monopod
63	24mm	1/2 @ f16	Velvia	Tripod
64	105mm	2 sec. @ f22	Velvia	Tripod
65	24mm	1 sec. @ f22	Velvia	Tripod
66	400mm	1/125 @ f8	Velvia	Monopod
67	400mm	1/125 @ f3.5	Velvia	Monopod
68-69	50mm	1/15 @ f16	Velvia	Tripod
70	105mm	1/2 @ f22	KR 64	Log
71	24mm	4 sec. @ f22	Velvia	Tripod
72	105mm & 27mm extension tube			
		1/4 @ f22	Velvia	Tripod
73	105mm	2 sec. @ f16	Velvia	Tripod
74	24mm	4 sec. @ f22	Velvia	Tripod
75	400mm	1/30 @ f3.5	Velvia	Tripod
76	400mm	1/8 @ f3.5	KR 64	Tripod
77	400mm	1/15 @ f8	Velvia	Tripod
78	105mm	1/15 @ f16	Velvia	Tripod
79	400mm	1/30 @ f3.5	Velvia	Tripod
80	400mm	1/250 @ f4	KR 64	Monopod
81	24mm	1/2 @ f16	Velvia	Tripod
82	105mm	1/30 @ f8	Velvia	Tripod
83	400mm & 27mm extension tube			
		2 sec. @ f16	Velvia	Tripod
84	400mm	1/125 @ f4	Velvia	Handheld
85	24mm	1 sec. @ f22	Velvia	Tripod
86	24mm	1/8 @ f22	Velvia	Ground
87	400mm	1/500 @ f3.5	KR 64	Handheld
88-89	400mm	1/30 @ f8	Velvia	Tripod
90	24mm	1/8 @ f22	Velvia	Tripod
91	105mm	1/30 @ f8	KR 64	Handheld
92	300mm	1/250 @ f4.5	KR 64	Handheld
93	400mm	1/125 @ f5.6	KR 64	Handheld
94	400mm	1/60 @ f5.6	Velvia	Stump
95	105mm	1/8 @ f11	Velvia	Tripod
96	300mm	1/250 @ f8	KR 64	Handheld
97	24mm	1/15 @ f22	Velvia	Tripod
98	105mm	1/30 @ f11	Velvia	Tripod
99	24mm	1/8 @ f22	Velvia	Tripod
100	24mm	1/4 @ f22	Velvia	Tripod
101	400mm	1/1000 @ f3.5	KR 64	Handheld
102	50mm	1/30 @ f16	Velvia	Tripod
103	300mm	1/500 @ f5.6	KR 64	Monopod
104	50mm	1/30 @ f22	Velvia	Tripod
105	400mm	1/250 @ f4	KR 64	Handheld
106	24mm	4 sec. @ f22	Velvia	Tripod
107	400mm	1/30 @ f3.5	Velvia	Tripod
108	105mm	1/15 @ f16	Velvia	Tripod
109	50mm	1/8 @ f22	Velvia	Tripod
110	105mm	1/60 @ f8	Velvia	Handheld
111	24mm	1/30 @ f8	Velvia	Handheld
112	400mm	1/15 @ f5.6	KR 64	Tripod
113	400mm	1/125 @ f4	Velvia	Handheld
114	50mm	2 sec. @ f22	Velvia	Tripod
115	400mm	1/90 @ f3.5	Velvia	Monopod
116	105mm	1/8 @ f16	Velvia	Tripod
117	24mm	1/30 @ f8	Velvia	Tripod
119	105mm	1 sec. @ f11	Velvia	Tripod
120	400mm	1/250 @ f8	KR 64	Tripod
121	300mm	1/125 @ f4.5	KR 64	Monopod
123	400mm	1/500 @ f4	KR 64	Handheld
124	24mm	1/15 @ f22	Velvia	Tripod
127	400mm	1/60 @ f3.5	Velvia	Tripod
128	50mm	1/125 @ f8	Fuji 50	Handheld

PARROT PITCHER PLANT BLOOMS
Stone County, May 1992

Appendix

State Parks

Buccaneer
1150 S. Beach Blvd.
Waveland, MS 39576

Casey Jones
P.O. Box 605
Vaughan, MS 39179

Clarkco
Rt. 1, Box 186
Quitman, MS 39355

Florewood River Plantation
P.O. Box 680
Greenwood, MS 38930

George P. Cossar
Rt. 1, Box 67
Oakland, MS 38948

Golden Memorial
Rt. 1, Box 8
Walnut Grove, MS 39189

Great River Road
P.O. Box 292
Rosedale, MS 38769

Holmes County
Rt. 1, Box 153
Durant, MS 39063

Hugh White
P.O. Box 725
Grenada, MS 38901

J. P. Coleman
Rt. 5, Box 504
Iuka, MS 38852

John W. Kyle
Rt. 1, Box 115
Sardis, MS 38666

Lake Lowndes
3319 Lake Lowndes Rd.
Columbus, MS 39702

LeFleur's Bluff
2140 Riverside Dr.
Jackson, MS 39202

Legion
Rt. 5, Box 32B
Louisville, MS 39339

Mississippi Department of Wildlife, Fisheries & Parks
P.O. Box 451
Jackson, MS 39205
(601)362-9212

MAGNOLIA AT SUNRISE
Issaquena County, May 1989

Leroy Percy
P.O. Box 176
Hollandale, MS 38748

Nanih Waiya
Rt. 3, Box 251-A
Louisville, MS 39339

Natchez
Rt. 5, Box 465
Natchez, MS 39120

Paul B. Johnson
Rt. 3, Box 408
Hattiesburg, MS 39401

Percy Quin
Rt. 3
McComb, MS 39648

Roosevelt
HCR 66, Box 33-D
Morton, MS 39117

Sam Dale
c/o Box 23093
Jackson, MS 39225-3093

Shepard
1034 Graveline Rd.
Gautier, MS 39553

Tishomingo
P.O. Box 880
Tishomingo, MS 38873

Tombigbee
Rt. 2, Box 336-E
Tupelo, MS 38801

Trace
Rt. 1, Box 254
Belden, MS 38826

Wall Doxey
Rt. 5, Box 245
Holly Springs, MS 38635

Winterville Mounds
Rt. 3, Box 600
Greenville, MS 38701

Lakes & Reservoirs

Kemper Lake
Kemper County
652 acres

Lake Lamar Bruce
Lee County
330 acres

Lake Monroe
Monroe County
111 acres

Lake Tom Bailey
Lauderdale County
234 acres

Lake Claude Bennett
Jasper County
71 acres

Lake Ross Barnett
Smith County
87 acres

Lake Mike Conner
Covington County
88 acres

Legion Lake
Simpson County
94 acres

Lake Dockery
Hinds County
55 acres

Lake Bogue Homa
Jones County
1200 acres

Lake Jeff Davis
Jefferson Davis County
164 acres

Lake Mary Crawford
Lawrence County
90 acres

Lake Bolivar
Bolivar County
512 acres

Lake Walthall
Walthall County
62 acres

Lake Columbia
Marion County
90 acres

Lake Bill Waller
Marion County
200 acres

Lake Perry
Perry County
125 acres

Oktibbeha County Lake
Oktibbeha County
479 acres

Reservoirs

Arklabutla
33,400 acres

Sardis
58,000 acres

Enid
28,000 acres

Grenada
63,000 acres

Ross Barnett
33,000 acres

Okatibbee
6,500 acres

MOCKINGBIRD
Hinds County, January 1986

Wildlife Management Areas & Refuges

Anderson-Tully
Rt. 2, Box 428
Rolling Fork, MS 39159

Bienville
Rt. 2, Box 82
Lena, MS 39094

Bucatunna
Rt. 1, Box 138
Quitman, MS 39355

Calhoun County
Box 354
Bruce, MS 38915

Caney Creek
Rt. 1, Box 150
Pulaski, MS 39152

Chickasaw
P.O. Box 18
Houlka, MS 38850
or
Rt. 4, Box 60-B
New Albany, MS 38652

Chickasawhay
P.O. Box 2245
Laurel, MS 39442-2245
or
P.O. Box 2743
Laurel, MS 39440

Choctaw
P.O. Box 639
Ackerman, MS 39735

Copiah County
Rt. 1, Box 83
Pattison, MS 39144

Divide Section
Rt. 1, Box 618
Golden, MS 38827

Homochitto
Rt. 3
Meadville, MS 39653

John Bell Williams
Rt. 3, Box 293
Booneville, MS 38829

Lake George
307 Lake Forest
Vicksburg, MS 39180

Leaf River
2841 Wire Rd.
Perkiston, MS 39573

Leroy Percy
Hollandale, MS 38748

Little Biloxi
Rt. 2, Box 126
Poplarville, MS 39470

Malmaison
Rt. 2, Box 220-A
Holcomb, MS 38940

Marion County
Rt. 2, Box 175
Columbia, MS 39429

Okatibbee Waterfowl Area
Rt. 3, Box 348
Collinsville, MS 39325

O'Keefe Waterfowl Area
115 Sweet Home Rd.
Belzoni, MS 39038

Old River
Rt. 1, Box 251-E
Poplarville, MS 39470

Pascagoula River
816 Wade-Vancleave Rd.
Pascagoula, MS 39567
or
Rt. 6, Box 350
Lucedale, MS 39452

Pearl River
462 East Sowell Rd.
Canton, MS 39046

Red Creek
129 Lafayette Circle
Ocean Springs, MS 39564

Sandy Creek
P.O. Box 215
Meadville, MS 39653

Shipland
Rt. 2, Box 428
Rolling Fork, MS 39159

John W. Starr Memorial Forest
304 Walnut Rd.
Starkville, MS 39759

Stoneville
115 Sweet Home Rd.
Belzoni, MS 39038

Sunflower
Box 261
Cary, MS 39054

Tallahala
Rt. 3, Box 547
Newton, MS 39345

Upper Sardis
Rt. 6, Box 189F
Oxford, MS 38655

Ward Bayou
19001 Larue Rd.
Ocean Springs, MS 39564

Wolf River
704 Church St.
Columbia, MS 39429

National Wildlife Refuges

Bogue Chitto
1010 Gause Blvd., Bldg. 936
Slidell, LA 70458

Hillside
Rt. 1, Box 286
Hollandale, MS 38748

Mathews Brake
Rt. 1, Box 286
Hollandale, MS 38748

Morgan Brake
Rt. 1, Box 286
Hollandale, MS 38748

Noxubee
Rt. 1, Box 84
Brooksville, MS 39739

Panther Swamp
Rt. 1, Box 286
Hollandale, MS 38748

Yazoo
Rt. 1, Box 286
Hollandale, MS 38748

Mississippi Sandhill Crane
7200 Crane Lane
Gautier, MS 39553

MALLARDS LEAVING FIELD
Tallahatchie County, December 1989

National Parks & Forests

U. S. Department of the Interior
National Park Service
3500 Park Road
Ocean Springs, MS 39564

Natchez Trace Parkway
Rt. 1, NT-143
Tupelo, MS 38801
(Includes many parks and natural areas along its 310-mile stretch)

Natchez National Historic Park
P.O. Box 1086
Natchez, MS 39121

Vicksburg National Military Park
3201 Clay Street
Vicksburg, MS 39180

Gulf Islands National Seashore
3500 Park Road
Ocean Springs, MS 39564

(Includes: Horn Island, East & West Ship Island, Petit Bois Island and Davis Bayou)

Mississippi National Forests
100 W. Capitol St., Suite 1141
Jackson, MS 39269

SUNFLOWERS & PINE TREES
Noxubee County, October 1992

Bienville National Forest
Bienville Ranger District
Rt. 2, Box 123-A
Forest, MS 39074

Strong River Ranger District
Box 217
Raleigh, MS 39153

Delta National Forest
Delta Ranger District
402 Hwy. 61 N.
Rolling Fork, MS 39159

DeSoto National Forest
Biloxi Ranger District
Rt. 1, Box 62
McHenry, MS 39561

Black Creek Ranger District
Box 428
Wiggins, MS 39577

Chickasawhay Ranger District
P.O. Box 426
Laurel, MS 39440

Holly Springs National Forest
Hwy 78 East, Box 400
Holly Springs, MS 38635

Homochitto National Forest
Bude Ranger District
Rt. 1, Box 1
Meadville, MS 39653

Homochitto Ranger District
Box 398
Gloster, MS 39638

Tombigbee National Forest
Tombigbee Ranger District
Rt. 1, Box 98-A
Ackerman, MS 39735

State Nursery
Ashe-Erambert Nursery
368 Ashe Nursery Road
Brooklyn, MS 39425

Hunting, Fishing & Outdoor Adventure

Archusa Creek Water Park
Rt. 4, Box 320
Quitman, MS 39355

Arkabutla Lake Field Office
U.S. Corps of Engineers
Rt. 1, Box 572
Coldwater, MS 38618

Batson's Catfish Farm & Red Creek Camping
1824 Hwy. 26 W.
Wiggins, MS 39577

Big Creek Water Park
Rt. 1
Soso, MS 39480

Black Creek Canoe Rentals
P.O. Box 414
Brooklyn, MS 39425

Bluff Creek Water Park
P.O. Box 5044
Vancleave, MS 39565

Bowie River Outdoor Sports
3552 Hwy. 42 West
Hattiesburg, MS 39402

Brannon & Brannon Hunts
Rt. 4, Box 455
Lucedale, MS 39452

Canemount Plantation
Rt. 2, Box 45
Lorman, MS 39096

Dry Creek Water Park
Rt. 3, Box 287
Mount Olive, MS 39119

Dunn's Falls
Rt. 1, Box 115
Enterprise, MS 39330

Flint Creek Water Park
1216 Parkway Dr.
Wiggins, MS 39577

Hide-A-Way Shooting Preserve
Rt. 1, Box 37
Lake, MS 39092

Indian Bluffs
c/o Holmes County Bank
316 Court Street
Lexington, MS 39095

Lake Tiak-O'Khata
P.O. Box 160
Louisville, MS 39339

Little Black Creek Water Park
Rt. 2, Box 34-D
Lumberton, MS 39455

Locopolis Lodge
306 North Market St.
Charleston, MS 38921

Longleaf Plantation
P.O. Box 511
Lumberton, MS 39455

Maynor Creek Water Park
P.O. Box 591
Waynesboro, MS 39367

McLeod Water Park
8100 Texas Flat Road
Bay St. Louis, MS 39525

Okatibbee Water Park
Rt. 12, Box 277
Meridian, MS 39301

Pelahatchie Creek Hunting Club
P.O. Box 122
Pelahatchie, MS 39145

Pond Store
Clark Creek Nature Area
182 Fort Adams Pond Road
Woodville, MS 39669

Presley's Outing
10501 Presley Outing Road
Pascagoula, MS 39581

Prospect Farms Shooting Preserve
Rt. 2, Box 602
Nettleton, MS 38858

Ship Island Excursions
P.O. Box 1467
Gulfport, MS 39502

Tara Wildlife
6971 Eagle Lake Shores Road
Vicksburg, MS 39180

Timberview Lodge
Rt. 1, Box 150
Porterville, MS 39352

Turkey Creek Water Park
Rt. 1, Box 100-A
Decatur, MS 39327

Webb's Camp
P.O. Box 576
Meadville, MS 39653

Wildlife Management, Inc.
45 Hillside Plantation Rd.
Natchez, MS 39120

Wildwood Hunt Club
P.O. Box 7
Benton, MS 39039

Bed & Breakfast Establishments

Anchuca Bed & Breakfast
1010 1st East St.
Vicksburg, MS 39180

Cedar Grove Bed & Breakfast Inn
2200 Oak Street
Vicksburg, MS 39180

Columbus Historic Foundation
P.O. Box 46
Columbus, MS 39703

The Duff Green Mansion & Bed & Breakfast
1114 1st East St.
Vicksburg, MS 39180

Gibson's Landing
1002 Church St.
Port Gibson, MS 39150

Hamilton Place Bed & Breakfast
330 South Hamilton
Holly Springs, Ms 38635

Homeplace Bed & Breakfast
P.O. Box 14
Poplarville, MS 39470

Natchez Pilgrimage Tours
P.O. Box 347
Natchez, MS 39121

Oak Square Plantation
1207 Church Street
Port Gibson, MS 39150

Southwind Guest House
337 S. Jackson
Houston, MS 38851

Education & Activity Centers

Batson's Log House & Museum
1862 Hwy. 26 W.
Wiggins, MS 39577

Crosby Aboretum
1801 Goodyear
Picayune, MS 39466

**Crow's Neck Environmental
Education Center**
281 County Road 115
Tishomingo, MS 38873

Grand Gulf Military Park
Rt. 2, Box 389
Port Gibson, MS 39150

J. L. Scott Marine Education Center
115 Beach Blvd.
Biloxi, MS 39531

**Mississippi Agriculture and
Forestry Museum**
1150 Lakeland Drive
Jackson, MS 39216

Mynelle Gardens
4736 Clinton Blvd.
Jackson, MS 39209

Natural Science Museum
111 North Jefferson Street
Jackson, MS 39202

Waterways Experiment Station
3909 Halls Ferry Road
Vicksburg, MS 39180-6199

Conservation Organizations & Agencies

Delta Wildlife Foundation
P.O. Box 276
Stoneville, MS 38776

**Mississippi Association of Conservation
Districts**
P.O. Box 23005
Jackson, MS 39225

Mississippi Cooperative Extension Service
P.O. Box 5446
Mississippi State, MS 39762

Mississippi Forestry Commission
301 N. Lamar Street, Suite 300
Jackson, MS 39201

Mississippi Wildlife Federation
P.O. Box 1814
Jackson, MS 39215

The Nature Conservancy
P.O. Box 1028
Jackson, MS 39215

Pat Harrison Waterway District
P.O. Drawer 1509
Hattiesburg, MS 39403

Pearl River Basin Development District
P.O. Box 5332
Jackson, MS 39296

Soil Conservation Service
100 West Capitol St., Suite 1321
Jackson, MS 39269-1399

For a complete 170-page guide to MISSISSIPPI
please write or call:

MISSISSIPPI TOURISM
P.O. Box 22825
Jackson, MS 39205-2825
1-800-647-2290

RUBY-THROATED HUMMINGBIRD AT CARDINAL FLOWER
Rankin County, September 1991

For more information on prints, books and
related materials contact:

Thy Marvelous Works
P.O. Box 31414
Jackson, MS 39286
601-362-7100

Epilogue

RAYS OF LIGHT IN THUNDERSTORM
Hinds County, June 1990

I want to take this opportunity to thank you for letting me share the preceding pages with you. I have truly enjoyed photographing wild Mississippi. The state's wealth of beauty is there for searching eyes and tender hearts. Something I found even more beautiful were its people. They invited me into their homes, fed me their food, showed me their secret places, and enriched my life with their conversations.

It is with a heart full of emotions that I close this wonderful chapter in my life. How could I ever really show you the Mississippi that is out there? The limitations of ink and paper make it impossible to bring forth the complete experience of Mississippi's outdoors. These 128 pages are not even enough to show all the photographs I have made. And on so many occasions, my eyes have taken in what the camera could not capture. In truth, of course, the bounty of the natural world is never fully revealed to the human eye.

So, in essence, in looking through these pages you have only seen a fraction of wild Mississippi. My hope is that my photographs will inspire you to wander the wilds on your own and often. As you go, I pray the Lord watch over and keep you. May He be a lamp unto your feet and light upon your path. It is then that the true wonder of *Wild Mississippi* will unravel before you.

Stephen Kirkpatrick
May 1993